DOGS
GONE BAD

JACK RUSSELL

amber
BOOKS

Published by
Amber Books Ltd
74–77 White Lion Street
London
N1 9PF
United Kingdom
www.amberbooks.co.uk
Appstore: itunes.com/apps/amberbooksltd
Facebook: www.facebook.com/amberbooks
Twitter: @amberbooks

ISBN: 978-1-78274-321-7

Project Editor: Sarah Uttridge
Designer: Keren Harragan
Picture Research: Terry Forshaw

Printed in China

Picture Credits
Alamy: 58 (Slim Plantagenate), 86 (Anni Sommer)
Depositphotos: 16 (RasulovS), 22 (Vitaly Titou & Maria Sidelnikova), 24 (Gsdonlin), 28 (Adogslifephoto), 30 (Photo-Deti), 32 (Igorr1), 36 (Olga Sweet), 38 (Chalabala), 40 (Andy Dean), 42 (Okssi 68), 46 (Boule 1301), 48 (Flydragonfly), 50 (Irin 717), 52 (RasulovS), 62 (Hannah Mariah), 64 top (Irstone), 68 top (Eppio), 70 (Avk78), 76 left (Bruno 135), 76 right (Feedough), 78 (Flydragonfly), 80 (J M Poget), 84 top (Builttospill), 84 bottom (Photo-Deti), 90 left (Cynoclub), 90 right (Marischka), 96 (Adogslifephoto)
Depositphotos/Damedeeso: 6, 8, 14, 18, 20, 26, 44, 56, 66, 74
Depositphotos/Willeecole: 12, 42, 82, 68 bottom, 88, 92
Fotolia: 54 (Annette Shaff), 60 (Shaun Hine), 64 bottom (Rita Kochmarjora)
Ingimage: 10, 72, 94

Contents

The Law's Got Paws

"I know, I know. Dog, donut, coffee, uniform. What's not to like?"

Too Much Bark, Too Little Bite

A dog that was scared of heights and loud noises was retired from service with the Cannon Beach Police Force in Oregon in 2014. Although Cash, a Belgian Malinois, had been trained, his timidity, unwillingness to jump into high places—such as to sniff out concealed drugs—and his tendency to bark nonstop rendered him useless as a police dog.

The Gym Bunny

"I'm known for my peek-a-bow-wow boxing technique."

Fat Camp

If the food we eat is good enough for us, then, some would say, it's good enough for our pets. So if going to the gym is good for us ... so it is for pets. Weight-loss spas have begun opening in the U.S. to deal with obese pets. Morris Animal Inn in New Jersey takes obese dogs (wearing life jackets) swimming and on runs to try to fight the flab.

Travelling In*dog*nito

"If you don't want to end up in a tin of dog food, don't ask no questions. If you lie down with dogs, you get fleas."

The Dog That Turned Its Coat

A dog that was once the protector of a senior Colombian drugs kingpin turned traitor in October 2014 when he began training to become a police dog. Confiscated when narcotics kingpin Cesar Martinez was arrested, Pecas—Spanish for "freckles"— was assigned to learn search-and-rescue missions at the police academy dog-training school.

Sick as a Dog

"The truth is, I look the same when I'm feeling great."

Festive Spirits

Like many of us, Tilly—a half Great Dane, half Rhodesian Ridgeback—indulged a little at Christmas. The difference is that she scarfed the whole Christmas cake, before being very sick. The cake, belonging to Tilly's owner Alison Cowell of Weymouth, UK, contained fruit soaked in alcohol, which damaged Tilly's liver and pancreas. Tilly had to be put on an intravenous drip and it took six weeks of medication before she was well again.

13

European Union

PET
PASSPO

Free to Rover

"I've got all the correct travel documents, but you've got to watch those cross-border collies."

Honestly, the Dog Ate It

"The dog ate my homework," may be a favorite children's excuse, but Russian ice-hockey player Anatoly Golyshev really can blame his dog for making him miss matches. Golyshev, who plays for Avtomobilist Yekaterinburg, returned home one day to find that his Yorkshire terrier had chewed up his passport. Golyshev was due to play international matches, but without an acceptable passport, he had to miss three weeks of games until a replacement was issued.

15

Ruff Justice

"Grr! In the doghouse again! And I thought they were only after cat burglars."

Mug Shot

Pep, a black labrador, was sentenced to life in Pennsylvania Penitentiary in 1924 for having murdered the governor's cat. A mug shot with prison number was even taken. His story was reported in the newspapers. He was framed, however. In fact, having been found chewing the governor's cushions, he was sent to the prison wings as a morale booster for the prisoners.

Watchdog

"Yes, you. I'm looking at you. You should feel flattered by the attention."

Lucky Black Dog

A lucky black dog in Fayetteville, Arkansas, managed to elude animal services 92 times in 2013 whenever it tried to catch it. Nicknamed LBD—Lucky Black Dog—he'll reappear nearby a few days later. "He runs around with friends," one local, Joan Threet, said. "Even if I'm walking my dog, he'll come up and harass my dog. He's brazen."

Cosmopolitan Canine

"Mine's a whisker sour."

Hair of the Dog

A man in East Helena, Montana, was arrested in 2012 after his dog was found to be four times over the drunk-driving limit. Harold Schrier, it was alleged, gave his Pomeranian vodka to drink. When the dog was found at Smith's Bar in East Helena, it was unable to stand. While Schrier was being held on a charge of cruelty to an animal, the dog went to an animal hospital. A humane society then took care of the dog.

Doggedly Undetermined

"Don't dog me—you're supposed to let sleeping dogs lie, remember? Besides, I regard it as the duty of man's best friend always to let my master win at chess."

Sleeping on the Job

A dozy guard dog was retired from a bar in Dartmouth, Devon, UK, in 2010, after he slept through their only burglary in 12 years. Raiders took hundreds of dollars worth of alcohol and stole cash from a quiz machine and donation boxes in the Dartmouth Arms pub while Taz slept. When staff arrived for work, Taz looked as pleased to see them as ever.

Pinching Doberman

"I'm a guard dog, me. Gardens, houses, but, above all, goals. Not just that, but if you thought dribbling was just about drool, think again. Problem is, sometimes I can get a bit carried away, and, well, I do like stealing the ball."

Pitch Invasion

In November 1970, a dog invaded a soccer game between English teams Colchester and Brentford. The dog collided with Chic Brodie, Brentford's goalkeeper, damaging ligaments in the goalie's knee. Colchester went on to win the game 4–0. Although Brodie returned to play a few more matches, the injury ended his professional soccer career.

Laptop Dog

"When I heard about the thousands of bites there were in computing, I thought that was the world for me. I've not found it as much fun as I'd anticipated, but I have electrocuted myself a few times."

Animal Magnetism

It might not seem strange that Polly, a cattle dog living in Victoria, Australia, had eaten a mouse, except that it was a computer mouse. But that's not all. She also ate 1000 small magnets, gardening gloves, a large rubber band, several rolls of fax paper, and handfuls of gravel—though not all in the same day. Over the years, she has cost her owner thousands of dollars in veterinarian and animal hospital bills.

Top Cat

As author Terry Pratchett said, "In ancient times cats were worshipped as gods; they have not forgotten this."

A Boy's Best Friend ... Is His Cat

In Bakersfield, California, in 2014, a boy was riding his tricycle when a neighbor's dog attacked him, biting his leg and trying to pull the boy off his bike. At that moment, the boy's pet cat sprang into action, jumping on the dog and chasing it off. The boy required stitches, the dog was put down, and the valiant cat was honored at a minor-league baseball game.

What Price My Love?

"I'll chew your newspaper, I'll chew your shoes, I'll bring you your purse. And in return, all I'll ask for is ... dog grooming, kennel stays, veterinary bills, and pet insurance."

Keeping the Change

A pug called Stella was admitted to an animal hospital in Albuquerque, New Mexico, in 2014. An abdominal exploration revealed that she had swallowed not one but 105 coins: 104 pennies and one quarter, making a total of—yes, quick counting, Lassie—$1.29. She recovered fine but left someone else to settle her medical bill.

I Love a Tumble

"Everyone knows that cleanliness is next to dogliness."

Missing: 43 Socks. Unmatched.

Retching when it was admitted to an animal hospital in Portland, Oregon, in 2014, a Great Dane was found to have eaten 43 and one-half socks. After surgery, the dog recovered. Although it was entered in a contest for weirdest things pets have eaten, the sock-eater only came third. Second place went to a dog that ate a whole kebab skewer, and first place to a frog that ate 30 ornamental rocks from its cage.

Yule Regret It

Pets aren't just for Christmas, and Christmas just isn't for some pets.

A Time for Giving—and Taking

It was in early December 2013 when Cato, a husky in South Carolina, took the Christmas spirit into his own paws. Having bolted from his owner's leash, he was spotted on a store's closed-circuit TV helping himself to some early presents—pig ears and treats—before nonchalantly leaving the premises. Followed outside, he led staff to a hole where he'd already buried some goodies. Stocking up for Christmas, it seems.

Doggy Snoop

"You know I'm tough. You can tell by the hat."

Bark but No Bite

When suspected drug dealers were arrested in Vargem Grande in southern Brazil in April 2015, their dog didn't charge at the police, nor did it escape to spread the word. Instead, when the suspects were made to lie down in a row, the dog joined them, even lying on its back and keeping its paws in the air—where the police could see them.

Wagging the Dog

"I do everything: check the trains, pack the bags, remember the leash. All he has to do is get to the station on time. And can he manage that?"

Leaps and Bounds

Thomas McCormack of North Lanarkshire, UK, knew that his collie-labrador mix Paddy couldn't climb over the 6ft (1.8m) garden fence. So how was it that the dog was waiting outside the front gate when he returned from work? And how did Paddy manage to pop up alongside Thomas on his train to work? In the yard was a trampoline on which Paddy would join Thomas's jumping children. It seems Paddy bounced his way over the fence and followed Thomas's scent to the station.

Doggone It

You might fret that Jack here can't see over the steering wheel or that his feet can't reach the pedals. But you're missing the point—he's not wearing a seat belt!

Offensive Driving

In 2006, a woman in China crashed her car while giving her dog a driving lesson. Mrs. Li said that her dog "was fond of crouching on the steering wheel," so she thought she'd let it "have a try." While she operated the accelerator and brake, the dog handled the wheel. They didn't make it far before crashing into an oncoming car.

Barking Boss

"When it comes to management-speak, I'm the best of the breed at getting all my ducks in a row."

Taxing Returns

What's the worst excuse you can come up with? When it comes to why people haven't filed their tax returns on time, Her Majesty's Revenue & Customs (the UK's tax agency) compiled a list of worst excuses with "My dog ate my tax return—and all the reminders" coming first. As Ruth Owen of HMRC said, "People can have a genuine excuse for missing a tax deadline, but owning a pet with a taste for HMRC envelopes isn't one of them."

Hangdog on a Telephone

"He's been missing for four hours ... Yes, brown, shorthair, usually friendly and energetic ... He's talkative, drives to work, plays golf, feeds me ..."

Chihuahua Chain Reaction

Lily, a Chihuahua in Tyneside, England, just wanted something to chew on when, one night in 2011, she grabbed the cell phone belonging to nine-year-old Aysha, who was sleeping nearby. Before Lily put the phone down, some of her saliva reached the phone's battery, causing it to heat up. This set the carpet alight, and the fire alarm went off. Aysha was quickly rescued by her mother, but by the time the fire truck arrived, the house was full of smoke.

Hush Puppy Money

"You know, I could explain how I got all this money, but you'd probably just call it a shaggy dog story."

Slumdog Millionaire

In a hotel room in the Indian state of Bihar in 2013, Nakched Mian left his money bag containing 400,000 rupees ($6,200) on his bed and went outside to wash his face. Noticing a stray dog had grabbed the bag, Mr. Mian approached the dog, but it ran away with the bag. Not quite all was lost; the dog had dropped 140,000 rupees on a street nearby.

Have Dog, Will Travel

"You think you're going to go on vacation leaving me here? Putting me in a kennel for a couple of weeks? Or having a neighbor walk me? You think I won't notice? You think I won't tear up the furniture? Wait and see."

Terrier Now Leaving from Gate K-9

Israel's Ben Gurion Airport in Tel Aviv is known for its emphasis on security, so it was a surprise when passengers on a 2013 London-bound British Airways flight noticed an unusual noise coming from one passenger's purse. The airplane was already on the runway, but returned to the terminal, where a Yorkshire terrier was found in the bag. Dog, luggage, and owner were removed from the flight.

I Think, Therefore I Chew

"For some, it's a pipe to smoke, for others, a glass of wine, but for me—if I really need to relax—it's got to be a shoe."

These Boots Weren't Made for Eating

Have you ever eaten a steak that tasted like shoe leather? So did a dog called Vince, but he didn't complain. He managed to devour a pair of calf-high, black women's boots belonging to his owner. Soon, though, the mixed-breed dog in Philadelphia was in discomfort and was admitted to an animal hospital. An X-ray showed a mass of shoe stuck in his stomach; even the boots' eyelets were visible. After surgery to remove the leather, Vince returned home.

Poodle and the Poulet

"There's nothing to be afraid about chickens coming home to roost. In fact, the very thought of it makes me hungry."

Dog's Dinner

The MacDonald family of Hamilton, New Zealand, were away from home when they received a call from a neighbor; a pitbull-mastiff was in their chicken coop. "This isn't going to end well," thought father Mark MacDonald as he turned the car around. Sure enough, the dog had climbed the 3ft (1m) fence, pulled away the wire from around the coop, and mauled to death the five hens that the family had owned for only six weeks. They didn't plan on getting any more.

Pug under Par

"Someone smarter than me once said that 'Golf is a good walk spoiled,' but aren't they one and the same? A game of golf—you know, digging holes, chasing balls, gnawing shoes—always involves a splendid walk, I find."

In the Ruff

Golfer Paul Casey was lining up for a putt on the twelfth green in the 2012 Dunhill Links Championship in St. Andrews, Scotland, when a small dog called Digby ran on to the green and off with his ball. Casey was about to play with a replacement ball when a spectator managed to retrieve the original ball from Digby, and an official allowed Casey to continue with that ball.

Who's Walking Whom?

"You think dressing me up in these boots is funny? I really hope you're not trying to provoke me into mauling another dog when we're out in the park, attacking a jogger, or scaring a child. I really hope you're not."

Dog Tired

Bobby, a seven-year-old mixed-breed spaniel, had the glory of being the 2015 winner of the Butcher's Fittest Dog contest in Britain. But there can be a downside to having such a healthy pet. He demands to be walked for seven hours a day. His owner, Sara Davis, was forced to leave her job working in the hospitality industry and become a professional dog walker to meet his needs.

The Bounder

"I can assure you that these feathers are from my pillow. How I acquired them for my pillow in the first place is another matter."

The Hunter and the Swan

The tranquility and beauty of the wetlands at Sudbury's common lands, a nature reserve, in East Anglia, UK, were shattered one day in March 2015 by a hunting dog. Before its owner could slip a leash on the dog, it bounded toward a swan as the bird was flapping its wings to take off. The swan was a moment too late, and the dog grabbed it in its jaws, killing it.

Jack Russell Terrier-ist

"Actually, I've only ever driven an automatic before, but I'm sure I'll be fine."

Driving Ambition

With his sheepdog Don, farmer Tom Hamilton drove his off-road pickup truck to inspect lambs on his farm in South Lanarkshire, UK, in April 2015. While examining a lamb, Mr. Hamilton saw the vehicle—with Don at the wheel—crashing through a fence, crossing the M74 motorway, and coming to a halt against the median. It seemed that Don had leaned on the controls, setting it in motion. Surprisingly, no one was hurt.

Bow-Wow-Ow

"Do you think the pet insurance company will believe us? Will they pay up?"

Canine Cons

If your dog doesn't want to walk any farther, it can do more than just refuse to move. A number of YouTube clips show dogs clearly faking injuries, such as dragging a foot or refusing to put pressure on a paw and hopping along as if it's lame. One dog even convincingly plays dead if he's picked up by anyone other than his owner.

One's Best Friend

"Buckingham Palace is my ancestral home. It must be; generations of corgis have lived here."

Royal Engagement

Every year, the British Royal Family gathers at the Queen's residence in Sandringham, Norfolk, for Christmas. The festive spirit was marred, though, in 2003. Within minutes of arriving, one of Princess Anne's bull terriers attacked one of the Queen's beloved corgis. The Princess and footmen pulled the dogs apart, but the corgi was so badly injured that it had to be put down. The bull terrier was spared.

It's Not a Yappy Day

"It's raining dogs and, er, those beasts I can't bear to name."

Noah's Dog

During a night at Northern Beaches Veterinary Hospital in Queensland, Australia, in 2014, a dog managed to get out of his pen and, while roaming around, turned on a faucet. By the following morning, there was quite a flood. Fortunately there was no serious damage, and the vet chose not to reveal the culprit's name to protect his identity.

Hot Dog

"You might look down on me, but have you ever felt the breeze in your face while hanging your head out of a speeding fire truck? Can you honestly tell me that you have? Because I do every day."

Fiery Treats

All Leo wanted was a dog biscuit. What he got was a fire that nearly burned down a house in London in April 2015. It's believed that in trying to reach some treats, Leo bumped a knob on the stove. The burner heated up a child's car seat that had been left there, causing a fire. As smoke began to fill the house, the son of the home's owner, his friend, and Leo escaped, but the kitchen was ruined.

With This Ring, I Thee Dog

"Bit of a diamond in the ruff, myself."

Expensive Tastes

With her fingers swollen due to her pregnancy, Nikki Balovich of Alaska took off her wedding ring. But then it disappeared. She suspected her mastiff Halli had swallowed it and that it would reappear when nature had taken its course. But this didn't happen. She'd given up hope of finding the ring when local residents clearing dog poop from a playing field spotted the glinting ring. A Facebook announcement soon helped the ring find its way back to Mrs. Balovich.

Distressed Furnishings

"I'm really torn up about what I've done."

Shabby Chic from a Shorthaired Pointer

Albert, a 12-month-old German Shorthaired pointer, was a busy pup in all the wrong ways. First, he grabbed a can of spray paint and decorated the walls of his home in Sydney, Australia, with black paint. Then, he dragged in bags of soil from the garden, leaving 6in (15cm) of dirt in the house. And, finally, he tore up two couches. Besides paying redecorating bills, his owners have now hired a dog guru.

Dog on Wheels

"Four legs good, two legs bad," they say. But what about "Four legs good, four wheels better"?

Wheels Come Off for Skateboarding Terrier

At one point, Bodhi was a YouTube sensation and appeared on TV on *Britain's Got Talent* with his skateboarding skills. But the Lakeland terrier, who wasn't trained to skateboard, caused his owner Jonathan Fell an £80 fine when two women tripped over his skateboard in Brighton, East Sussex, UK, in 2011. The local court also threatened to order Fell to keep the pooch from his wheel tricks.

Howl Loud is My Bark?

"I don't know what she's complaining about—most people can't even hear dog whistles."

Barking Judgment

A woman in Seattle, Washington, was in danger of losing her home in 2015 after a neighbor brought a lawsuit against her because of her noisy dog. The neighbor claimed that even through double-glazed windows, the sound of Cawper's barking reached 128 decibels—as loud as a chainsaw. Cawper's owner, Denise Norton, had thought the lawsuit was a joke and had ignored it. By failing to appear in court, however, she automatically lost the case and was told to pay the neighbor $500,000 in damages.

Love Me, Love My Dog

"Someone's been sleeping in my bed," said Baby Bear, "and they're still there!"

Pillow Fight

A woman from Monmouthshire, UK, thought that her three-year-old son was autistic because of his violent temper tantrums. The cause, however, was something canine. Robyn, Billy's mother, allowed Billy to be examined for a TV documentary about child behavior. A team of experts monitored Billy's sleep and found that the pet dog was stealing Billy's pillow, disrupting the boy's crucial sleeping patterns. Billy was not autistic at all but sleep deprived!

Cool Drool

*"I don't wear them to look cool. It's just that my eyes are very sensitive to the sun, bright lights, and the *pup*arazzi."*

Don't Be Seen without Them

What do you always need with you when you leave the house? Keys, money, phone ... sunglasses? This became non-negotiable for Fei Fei in Chongqing, central China, in 2009. Once owner Bo Lee had given Fei Fei sunglasses to wear to protect him from the sun, the dog refused to leave the house again without them. "If I try to leave the apartment without them, he howls the place down," Bo Lee said.

Crying Waterfowl

"Damn it, the duck's beaten me again! I keep blinking first."

Wade in the Water

To what extremes do you go to retrieve your dog? After a dog chased a duck and her ten ducklings into a pond on Outwood Common in Surrey, UK, in 2015, its owner spent half an hour calling it back. But the dog ignored her and continued chasing the ducks around the pond. Finally, the woman had to resort to more drastic measures. She waded chest deep into the middle of the pond, grabbed her dog by its ear, and dragged it out.

Gone to the Dogs

"I know, I know, I've made a real paw job of that panel-beating."

Pack Mentality

Finding a stray dog lying in his parking spot in 2015, a man in Chongqing in southwest China kicked it, sending it on its way. Minutes later, when the man had gone, the dog returned with two of its pack. They started chewing up the car's hubcaps and windshield wiper, but have kept away since their revenge.

Paper Shredder

"I'm very efficient at recycling paper. I start the moment I take the mail out of the mailbox."

Postal Disorder

For more than four months in 2014, letters were not delivered to a street in Sandiacre, Nottingham, UK, because the postman had been bitten by a German Shepherd dog that lived there. The postman said, "I've got puncture marks on my elbow and one on my back. I'm not frightened of dogs, but it has changed my whole perception of them."

The Dogs of War

"If dogs weren't meant to go into battle, why do all soldiers wear dog tags? I say that every underdog will have its day."

Let Sleeping Grenades Lie

You might think that the worst thing your dog could bring home would be a mauled animal. But what about a live hand grenade? While Stefan Bojanowski was walking his 15-year-old labrador Jake near Holt, Norfolk, UK, in 2005, the dog bounded off into bushes to re-emerge proudly gripping a World War II grenade between its teeth. Recognizing what it was, Mr. Bojanowski left the grenade on the track and called the police. Bomb disposal experts later detonated the device.

Behind Closed Paws

"You think when I gaze at you lovingly, follow you around all day, and put that ever-so-innocent look on my face when you're locking the doors that I'm not actually choosing the moment to make my break?"

Who Let the Dogs Out?

For a time in 2007, staff at London's Battersea Dogs & Cats Home would arrive for work to find one corridor of dog kennels all open and the dogs wandering around freely. Unable to work out how the dogs had escaped, they installed closed-circuit TV cameras. From these, they learned that one dog managed to pull back the bolt on his kennel, run to the kitchen for a quick snack, and then release his friends from other kennels for a midnight feast.

Why the Long Face?

"Who says I don't look cute in a cheerleader's skirt?"

Lapdog of Honor
At the 2010 Commonwealth Games in Delhi, India, a dog bounded into the stadium as officials were preparing for a women's 400 meter hurdle qualifying heat. The dog raced the length of the stadium, dodging anyone who tried to catch it. After its moment in the spotlight, the dog found its way to an exit.

Bad Dog

"They've threatened to put me down, but I'm not scared—I can take a few patronizing comments."

New Tricks

For some the word *Cats* is a musical, but for Big Fella, a bull mastiff cross, the word meant "Attack!" When a police officer visited the home of Robert Harper one night in Manchester, UK, in 2005, Harper tried to flee the scene, using his "Cats" code word to instruct Big Fella to attack the police officer. Despite several bites to his arms that later required hospital treatment, the officer managed to hold on to both Harper and Big Fella. Harper later received a jail sentence for assault.